Alfred's ROCK Ed. | CLASSIC ROCK DRUMS Vol. 1

LEARN ROCK BY PLAYING ROCK

mp3

The included CD-ROM contains sound-alike and play-along MP3s of each song, as well as MP3s of the instructional examples found throughout the song lessons. To access these recordings, insert the CD-ROM into a computer, double-click on My Computer, right-click on the CD drive icon, and select Explore. (Mac users can simply double-click the CD icon that appears on the desktop.) The MP3s are located in the "**MP3s**" folder.

TNT 2 CUSTOM MIX

In addition to the MP3s, the CD-ROM contains our exclusive TNT 2 software that you can use to alter the instrument and vocal mixes of the song recordings, loop playback, and change keys and tempos.

For installation, follow the instructions at left to explore the disc and double-click on the installer file. Installation may take up to 15 minutes.

PDF Adobe

For your convenience, the CD-ROM also contains PDFs of the vocal parts to the three songs taught in this book. To access the PDFs, follow the MP3 instructions to explore the disc and proceed to the "**Vocal Parts**" folder.

TNT 2 SYSTEM REQUIREMENTS

Windows
7, Vista, XP
1.8 GHz processor or faster
650 MB hard drive space, 2 GB RAM minimum
Speakers or headphones
Internet access required for updates

Macintosh
OS 10.4 and higher (Intel only)
650 MB hard drive space, 2 GB RAM minimum
Speakers or headphones
Internet access required for updates

Produced by
Alfred Music Publishing Co., Inc.
P.O. Box 10003
Van Nuys, CA 91410-0003
alfred.com

Printed in USA.

ISBN-10: 0-7390-9320-7 (Book & CD-ROM)
ISBN-13: 978-0-7390-9320-7 (Book & CD-ROM)

Recordings
Guitars: John Allen • Bass: Albert Nigro • Keyboards: Ethan Neuburg • Drums: Nicholas Neuburg

CONTENTS

FOREWORD

Rock is a small-group art. It's about playing together—guitar, bass, keys, and drums locked into a tight groove, hammering away on a relentless riff while functioning as one seamless rhythm section. Many music schools are now teaching in a rock group format in addition to, or even instead of, individual private lessons, because it is in the group format that we really learn to rock.

Alfred's Rock Ed. series presents many of the greatest rock songs of all time in professionally arranged guitar, bass, keyboard, and drum folios for beginning and intermediate rock bands. This series is perfect for schools that teach students to perform together in a rock band and for individuals looking to start their own garage band. Each instrument-specific folio includes parts, the full score, instruction, a CD-ROM with MP3s, and our exclusive TNT 2 software!

LEARNING WITH THE MP3s AND TNT2 CUSTOM MIX SOFTWARE

As you work your way through the song lessons, you'll notice numbered disc icons throughout the lesson examples and instrument parts. Most of the examples have been recorded at-tempo and also at a slower speed so you can really hear what's going on. And every song has a corresponding sound-alike recording and play-along track (minus the instrument) so you can jam along with a professional band—if you don't already have a band of your own. These recordings are invaluable as you learn to play in a group—they're basically a road map for how you should sound as you improve at your instrument.

The TNT 2 software gives you even more options: you can alter the instrument and vocal mixes of every song to hear how the parts work together, slow tracks down for in-depth listening, loop sections to focus in on a part, and even change keys (perfect for vocal practice)!

For instructions on accessing the MP3s, installing the TNT 2 Custom Mix software, and system requirements, refer to page 1.

COMMUNICATION BREAKDOWN

"Communication Breakdown" was the B-side of the first single from Led Zeppelin's self-titled debut album released in January 1969. The British band emerged from the ashes of the recently defunct Yardbirds when guitarist Jimmy Page and vocalist Robert Plant invited bass and keyboard session player John Paul Jones and a young powerhouse drummer named John Bonham to join their band. The name "Led Zeppelin" was intended to exemplify the combination of heaviness and light (electric and acoustic) that the members wished to explore. But there is very little "light" in a driving rocker like "Communication Breakdown."

THE CD-ROM: In addition to the sound-alike and play-along MP3s, all music examples are provided on the disc. Use the CD-ROM to carefully listen to your parts and practice along. Also, with the included TNT 2 software, you can alter the instrument and vocal mix, slow tracks down, and loop sections for practice.

VERSE: Below is the two-bar pattern for the verse. In the first measure, keep a steady quarter-note pulse on the hi-hat, with the snare on beats 2 and 4, and the bass drum filling in on the eighth notes in between the snare hits. In the second measure, the kick and crash cymbal accent the "&" of 1 and beat 3 along with the bass and guitars. Don't forget that little eighth-note pickup on the kick before beat 3.

TRACK 1
At-tempo

TRACK 2
Slow

The two-bar pattern written above is the one that Bonham used for live performances (and is also what's used in our sound-alike recording), with the crash cymbal on the "&" of beat 1 of the second measure, and quarter notes on 3 and 4. The example below is the pattern used on the classic recording. Notice the slight variation in the second measure, with no crash on beat 4, but a flamed snare instead.

TRACK 3
At-tempo

CHORUS: The chorus is a repeated four-bar pattern with quarter-note hi-hat, snare on beats 2 and 4, the bass drum playing the eighth notes in between snare hits, and the crash cymbal adding emphasis to the guitar accents on the "&" of 4.

TRACK 4
At-tempo

TRACK 5
Slow

GUITAR SOLO: The drum pattern remains exactly as it was for the verse. The guitar solo is slightly shorter than the verse: 14 measures instead of 16.

CODA AND END: The same as the verse pattern, and the song ends exactly on the last beat of the two-measure pattern.

COMMUNICATION BREAKDOWN

Words and Music by JIMMY PAGE,
JOHN PAUL JONES and JOHN BONHAM

Communication Breakdown - 3 - 1

Verse 2:
Hey, babe, I got something I think you ought to know.
Hey, babe, I wanna tell you that I love you so. I wanna hold you in my arms, yeah!
I'm never gonna let you go, 'cause I like your charm.
(To Chorus:)

Communication Breakdown - 3 - 3

GIMME SOME LOVIN'

In the mid-'60s, while a teenage "Little" Stevie Wonder was tearing up the charts from under the Motown umbrella, another prodigy multi-instrumentalist/vocalist was gaining notoriety from the midlands of England. Steve Winwood was adding impassioned Ray Charles-style vocals, gritty blues guitar, and screaming organ to tracks from both The Spencer Davis Group and, later, Traffic. "Gimme Some Lovin'" (1966) was The Spencer Davis Group's biggest hit on both sides of the Atlantic and has been covered innumerable times, featured in dozens of film soundtracks and commercials, and remains a staple of Steve Winwood's live repertoire to date.

THE CD-ROM: In addition to the sound-alike and play-along MP3s, all music examples are provided on the disc. Use the CD-ROM to carefully listen to your parts and practice along. Also, with the included TNT 2 software, you can alter the instrument and vocal mix, slow tracks down, and loop sections for practice.

INTRO: The signature bass riff that kicks off the song consists of alternating octaves and was inspired by the Homer Banks record "A Lot of Love" (look it up on YouTube).

Notice in the transcription that the first two measures of the drums (with repeats) are mostly a low tom, with kick and hi-hat accents on beat 4.

TRACK 8
At-tempo

TRACK 9
At-tempo

The full pattern then enters on measure 3, with the low tom still accenting beat 4

TRACK 10
Slow

VERSE: During the verses, the drums continue to hold down the steady four on the hi-hat with a bass drum and snare pattern that is duplicated by the bass guitar.

PRE-CHORUS: The four-measure pre-chorus continues with a similar pattern and a gradual crescendo into the chorus. Add a crash cymbal on beat 1 of each measure for a new dynamic.

TRACK 11
At-tempo

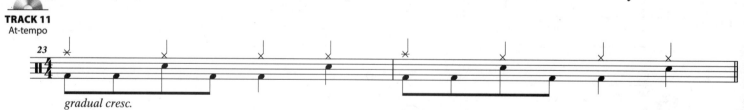

gradual cresc.

CHORUS: The same basic pattern is used with more intensity. But a new variation is added with the crash on beat 1 of *every other* measure.

CODA: The coda is really an extended chorus. Feel free to add a little variation to the pattern to make it more exciting as shown below.

The song concludes with another crescendo over the pre-chorus chord progression, ending in a furious fermata fill and a tutti smack, meaning everyone hits their note or chord together at once.

END: When playing with a band, the fermata (held note) normally ends on a visual cue. To get a clean ending on the recording, we have made the value of this fermata exactly eight beats, but when playing live someone in the band should signal the end of the fermata. Feel free to go wild here, building up to the final hit on the last note.

Here is the fill we've used, but again, you should make this your own.

GIMME SOME LOVIN'

Words and Music by STEVE WINWOOD,
MUFF WINWOOD and SPENCER DAVIS

Gimme Some Lovin' - 2 - 1

Gimme Some Lovin' - 2 - 2

MONEY

Having sold more than 200 million albums, Pink Floyd is one of the most successful rock bands in history, but ironically, "Money" has the distinction of being one of only two top 20 singles the group ever released.

Roger Waters' acoustic demo recording of the song reveals he had the song's shifting time signatures of 7/4 to 4/4 to 6/4 and back to 7/4 right from the get-go. Guitarist David Gilmour's contribution includes the deftly orchestrated electric guitars.

THE CD-ROM: In addition to the sound-alike and play-along MP3s, all music examples are provided on the disc. Use the CD-ROM to carefully listen to your parts and practice along. Also, with the included TNT 2 software, you can alter the instrument and vocal mix, slow tracks down, and loop sections for practice.

INTRO/VERSE: Don't be intimidated by the odd meter of 7/4. Most of "Money" is played as a two-bar pattern of a basic backbeat with the final beat (the last snare hit) omitted. Simply count 1, 2, 3, 4, 1, 2, 3; 1, 2, 3, 4, 1, 2, 3; etc. But don't get too hung up on counting or you'll lose the easy swing of the tune.

The drum pattern uses crash accents on beats 1 and 7. This really helps delineate the beginning and end of each measure.

Below is a part of the verse pattern, shown in 7/4.

TRACK 16
At-tempo

Alternatively, here's the main part notated as a combination of a bar of 4/4 and a bar of 3/4.

TRACK 17
At-tempo

The two bars leading up to the guitar solo build by using eighth-note triplets on the snare drum. In our sound-alike recording and in this example, these triplets were played on the snare, but feel free to change it to the toms if you desire. This pattern is repeated at the end of the guitar solo as well.

TRACK 18
At-tempo

TRACK 19
Slow

GUITAR SOLO: The guitar solo is all in $\frac{4}{4}$. The drum pattern is a continuation of the eighth-note triplets, now on the hi-hat, with a fairly standard kick and snare pattern. Note the juxtaposition of the triplet eighth notes on the hi-hat with the straight eighth notes on the kick drum on beat 3. For this example, the triplets are all played on the hi-hat, but for variation try the ride or crash on the first beat of each measure.

.ACK 20
:-tempo

.ACK 21
Slow

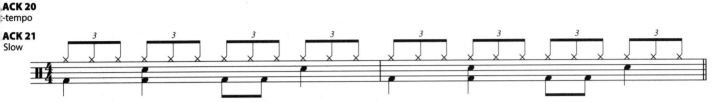

END: After the last verse, the song goes into a new $\frac{4}{4}$ pattern, with a ride cymbal playing all four beats. Remember to keep it swinging.

.ACK 22
:-tempo

There is a fermata (held note) on beat 3 of the second-to-last measure.

Normally when performing with a band these notes are played and held to a visual cue, but in order to get a clean ending on the recording, we have made it exactly six beats.

MONEY

Words and Music by ROGER WATERS

Moderately ♩ = 120

Intro:

Verses 1 & 2:

1. Mon-ey, ya get a - way. Ya get a good job with more pay, and you're o -
2. Mon-ey, you get back. I'm all right, Jack, keep your hands off my

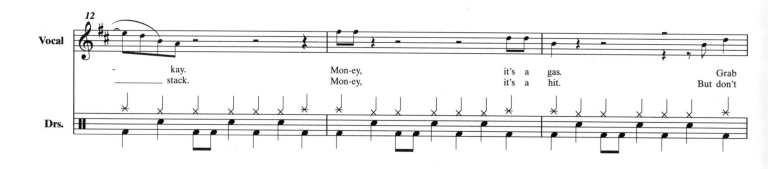

- kay. Mon-ey, it's a gas. Grab
- stack. Mon-ey, it's a hit. But don't

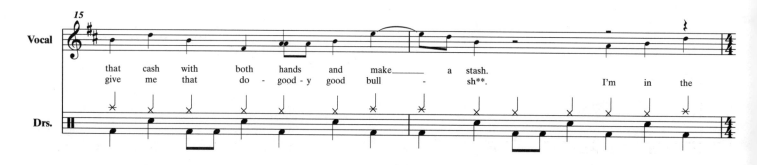

that cash with both hands and make a stash. I'm in the
give me that do - good - y good bull - sh**. I'm in the

Money - 6 - 1

Money - 6 - 3

Verse 3:

TRACK 6
Sound-alike

COMMUNICATION BREAKDOWN
(Score)

Words and Music by JIMMY PAGE,
JOHN PAUL JONES and JOHN BONHAM

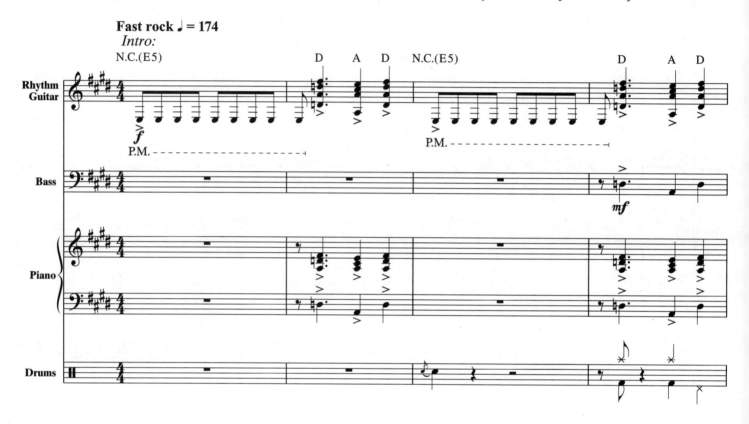

Communication Breakdown - 8 - 1

%*Chorus:*

Com-mu - ni - ca - tion break - down,__ it's al-ways the same.__

Hav-ing a ner - vous break - down,__ drive me in - sane.____

Communication Breakdown - 8 - 4

*Cont. ad lib. w/E minor pentatonic
and E major pentatonic scales*

D.S. 𝄋 al Coda

Communication Breakdown - 8 - 6

Communication Breakdown - 8 - 8

TRACK 14
Sound-alike

GIMME SOME LOVIN'
(Score)

Words and Music by STEVE WINWOOD,
MUFF WINWOOD and SPENCER DAVIS

Gimme Some Lovin' - 6 - 1

Gimme Some Lovin' - 6 - 3

Gimme Some Lovin' - 6 - 4

Gimme Some Lovin' - 6 - 5

Gimme Some Lovin' - 6 - 6

TRACK 23
Sound-alike

MONEY
(Score)

Words and Music by ROGER WATERS

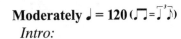

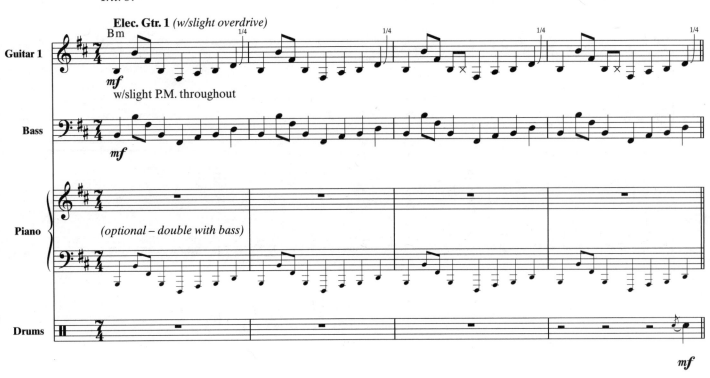

Money - 14 - 1

Sax Solo:

Money - 14 - 7

Money - 14 - 10

Verse 3:

Outro:

a - way,_____ a - way,_____ a - way,_____ a - way,_____

a - way._____

decresc.

decresc.

decresc.

decresc.

decresc.

Money - 14 - 13

Money - 14 - 14